Pathfinder 35

On course for GCSE coursev

The *Pathfinder* Series

All **Pathfinders** are available through
good book suppliers or direct from:
Central Books, 99 Wallis Rd,
London E9 5LN. Tel: 0845 458 9910
(mail order line). Fax: 0845 458 9912.
Book trade representation (UK and
Ireland): **Broadcast Book Services,**
Charter House, 27a London Rd, Croydon
CR0 2RE. Tel: 020 8681 8949.
Fax: 020 8688 0615.

Pathfinder 35

A CILT series for language teachers

On course for GCSE coursework

2nd edition

Julie Adams

Centre for Information
on Language Teaching and Research

The views expressed in this publication are the author's and do not necessarily represent those of CILT, the examination boards or curriculum bodies mentioned.

Acknowledgements

I would like to repeat my thanks to all those acknowledged in the first edition, but I am also indebted to the following:

Mustafa Azmi, Belle Vue Boys' School, Bradford
Sarah Cartwright, London Metropolitan University
Rebecca Munslow, St Paul's School for Girls, Edgbaston
Kanta Shah, (formerly) Whitmore High School, Harrow
Marg Whiffin, Wilnecote High School, Tamworth

First published 1998 by the Centre for Information on Language Teaching and Research (CILT), 20 Bedfordbury, London WC2N 4LB. Second edition 2002

ISBN 1 904243 06 1

A catalogue record for this book is available from the British Library

Printed in Great Britain by Cromwell Press Ltd

CILT Publications are available from: **Central Books,** 99 Wallis Rd, London E9 5LN. Tel: 0845 458 9910. Fax: 0845 458 9912. Book trade representation (UK and Ireland): **Broadcast Book Services,** Charter House, 27a London Rd, Croydon CR0 2RE. Tel: 020 8681 8949. Fax: 020 8688 0615.

Contents

Introduction

 ## WHY DO COURSEWORK?

Only four years after the original publication of *On course for GCSE coursework* it has become necessary to revise this book. This is partly a result of the changed requirements in GCSE MFL examinations from 2003, and these new requirements are fully covered here. However, my main reason for updating this *Pathfinder* is that teachers have taken coursework to their hearts and made an undoubted success of it. In my various roles as a moderator, researcher, coursework adviser and CPD provider, I have been privileged to work with talented teachers throughout the United Kingdom and to read the impressive and interesting coursework of thousands of GCSE students. Students write on subjects as diverse as imaginative responses to songs, simple historical accounts of the target language country and analyses of adverts from the target language media. They incorporate their previous experience, they attempt a variety of genres and produce impressive target language. I am delighted to be associated with GCSE coursework as I remain firmly convinced (and my research has also shown) that coursework contributes to improved standards in MFL (not just in writing either) and gives students opportunities to engage in areas previously excluded from some GCSE syllabuses.

> *'The motivation factor of coursework is a significant consideration for students. Some young people respond better when they know the assignment they are working on might count towards the "real exam". You will recognise the plaintive cry: "I couldn't do my French homework because I had to finish my Geography coursework." Why shouldn't French have its turn?'*
> (Jackie Coe, 'What's right for writing – coursework or exam?' *TES* 19.10.2001)

This book looks at what coursework means for Modern Languages and how it differs from other subjects. Of major importance in achieving success in coursework is effective preparation, and various approaches to this are proposed. Guidance is given on what exactly the exam boards require and how these requirements can be communicated to the students. The need to prepare the ground for good coursework in Key Stage 3 and writing for bilingual students are discussed. Finally, there is a chapter on trouble-shooting. The text is illustrated throughout with exemplar materials and extracts from students' written work. Comments have been added to students' work to help in gaining an appreciation of the issues involved in coursework, rather than marking them according to exam board criteria. The book covers the requirements for coursework in writing of all the major exam boards in the United Kingdom, i.e. AQA Specification A, AQA Specification B (Module 3), Edexcel, OCR, WJEC and writing for the Scottish Standard Grade (see Appendix page 41) for a summary of the arrangements for writing assessment of each board).

1. What does 'coursework' mean for Modern Languages?

Assessment by coursework has many advantages and in many aspects the GCSE coursework requirements reflect existing good practice. Coursework allows the teaching and assessment processes to support each other, rather than assessment having to be completely separated from normal classroom activity.

It is helpful to use John Thorogood's analogy of the 'Teaching and learning train' when conceptualising coursework: students will be doing very similar pieces of written work to normal classroom good practice, but we (their language teachers) will just be going off 'on a branch line' to collect this work in a different way and present it as part of the GCSE. Very often this written work is of a type that KS4 students would regularly be writing and that their teachers would be marking.

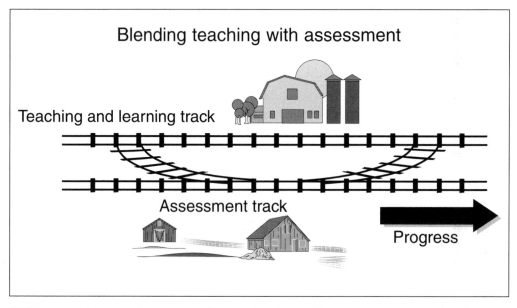

While we can learn much from our colleagues in other subjects, we must have a clear idea that Modern Languages coursework will be different from the projects and investigations carried out for GCSE coursework in other curriculum areas. This is because the nature of teaching and learning in our subject is very different and we must find ways to communicate the differing requirements and outcomes of this learning process to our students. Although experience of MFL coursework at AS and A level will be helpful experience, this should also not lead us to unrealistic expectations of coursework at GCSE level.

The title 'coursework' sounds intimidating and very official and it may be more helpful for Modern Languages teachers to think of GCSE coursework as a series of periodic, short assessments in writing. These are just some of the ways in which coursework in Modern Languages is different to coursework in many other subjects:

- the pieces of writing are comparatively short – usually about 150 words;

- in Modern Languages coursework all students are likely to be writing about the same subject, using very similar language;

- the teacher may present new material, e.g. new structures, before the students start to write, therefore the piece of writing is more likely to be close to the teacher's model;

- coursework in Modern Languages is less likely to be a long-term piece of work requiring independent research – the deadline between setting the coursework and completion is likely to be days at the most;

- students are less likely to be using a large number of source materials.

ADVANTAGES OF COURSEWORK

One of the main advantages of coursework is that the board's requirements can be implemented in the way which best suits your local conditions. The teachers quoted here demonstrate this strength by describing variety in patterns of coursework provision:

> *'We do coursework with all our students in all the languages we teach. They can't do coursework when we enter them for GCSEs in other community languages because we can't supervise them effectively and sometimes coursework isn't offered in those languages (e.g. Bengali).'*

> *'We do coursework with all our candidates except the most able – they already have a lot of coursework in their other subjects and we tend to find they do just as well in the terminal writing exam, probably for less effort.'*

> *'We do coursework with everyone in French, but not in German or Italian which they usually do as second languages. We just thought that coursework in two languages was a bit too much for them.'*

> *'As our students are adults we offer them the choice of coursework or the terminal paper. Most are very quick to see the advantage of coursework and opt for it! They take it very seriously indeed and do three pieces of work under controlled conditions. Sometimes if they think they can improve their score they do an extra piece independently at home.'*

> *'Only the bottom set does coursework. We choose tasks which mean they can use lots of ICT and illustration and they really enjoy it. Sometimes some of them get a GCSE grade from their coursework alone.'*

If your department is still at the stage of deciding whether or not you should do coursework, you may like to discuss the following points together and see how many of these advantages apply to your students:

- Good performance in writing coursework is less reliant on memory (and luck in the questions that appear on the paper!) than a terminal examination; the higher tier writing paper in the GCSE has instructions in the target language, which may make it more 'difficult' or intimidating.

- There is greater scope in coursework for students to write on a subject which interests them, rather than the usual narrower range of transactional tasks suitable for an exam context.

- For most boards the assessment criteria are similar to the existing criteria for GCSE writing papers, so teachers will be able to mark written coursework assignments in a similar way, for example, to previous 'mock exams'.

- Coursework written under 'controlled conditions' can be a suitable task for end-of-year or mock exams.

- There is no fixed amount of time for students to write each piece of coursework, so it is easier to allow them to work at their own pace; also, all boards permit candidates to write coursework throughout the GCSE course and the best three pieces (five for WJEC) to be selected for submission.

- Coursework lightens 'Year 11 exam load' by replacing the terminal writing exam; coursework is completed well before Easter in the year of the examination so leaving extra time to prepare for the oral and other terminal papers.

- Students who do not complete the required number of pieces of coursework can still be entered for the terminal exam in writing at a comparatively late stage (centres can have some of their candidates entered for coursework and others doing the terminal exam).

- Coursework allows Modern Languages to have parity with other subjects in Key Stage 4, so that students apply themselves regularly to Modern Languages work.

- The effective coursework process allows the teacher to give regular, constructive feedback to students.

CiLT

- Students tend to be motivated knowing that they have already gained a particular grade before they even start the exams at the end of Year 11.

- GCSE coursework lays the foundations for a confident approach to coursework in the new A level specifications.

It is clear that coursework offers many possibilities, both for imaginative work and for candidates to perform at their best level of achievement. Coursework allows a wider range of activities to be sampled and assessed than is possible in a terminal examination.
OCR GCSE Specification

WHAT ELSE DO WE NEED TO DISCUSS?

Taking on the assessment for part of the GCSE clearly carries responsibility with it and colleagues need to be clear about this before starting coursework. There is a small amount of exam-related administration required from each class teacher, mostly noting marks and storing coursework securely. Many teachers believe that writing coursework increases the markload, but this shouldn't be the case unduly as, in the long run, teachers will only be marking work similar to the usual writing tasks set in each topic throughout KS4.

NB Edexcel, OCR and WJEC offer centres the opportunity to assess their own oral exams. This option may not be chosen if the centre is submitting writing coursework. Centres need not usually make a final decision about entry for coursework or terminal writing papers until final entries are submitted. It is also usually possible to change entry after this point (i.e. swap from coursework to the terminal exam) on payment of an extra fee.

I leave the final word on 'terminal exam versus coursework' to a Principal Moderator:

> *'The difference between the exam and coursework is that they **learn** from the written coursework they ultimately submit for the exam, they learn from the process.'*

2. Effective preparation for coursework

A Chief Examiner for coursework in another curriculum subject states:

> *'We wouldn't send students into an exam to write their first ever essay, and yet I regularly see pieces of coursework where it is obvious that this is the first time that they have written any coursework.'*

The implication is that we should give students the opportunity to practise their writing, in the same way that we give them the opportunity to practise their speaking before the oral exam. But how can we achieve this without compromising the exam boards' guidelines on teacher intervention and fairness?

The question I am most often asked about coursework by MFL teachers is: 'How much help I am allowed to give?' The short answer is: 'As much help as you like.' However, any support given for a writing task must be taken into consideration at the marking stage. This means that those candidates who find the writing most difficult can be given writing frames, highly structured support sheets and detailed planning sessions while the most confident writers can be given the task and left to complete the coursework pretty much unaided. However, whatever the ability level of the candidates it is expected that they will have been taught the relevant language before tackling the coursework, which includes practice in all four skills – including writing! The following diagram helps to illustrate the relationship between the amount of help given and the marks awarded:

SUPPORT GIVEN AT FINAL WRITING STAGE

CREDIT AWARDED FOR INDEPENDENT WRITING

▲ GRADE G   GRADE A* ▲

 BUILDING UP TO THE COURSEWORK TASK

It is advisable to ask students to write only on language areas which are familiar to them. This means that any writing should usually be left until towards the end of a topic, after they have encountered any new language or structures in listening, speaking and reading.

It is clear that the most successful coursework is integrated into a teaching unit in the KS4 scheme of work. In other words, coursework **shouldn't** be regarded as a 'bolt-on' extra handled in a very different way to normal classroom work. Most pieces of standard coursework such as writing an account of a holiday or writing about work experience lend themselves well to integration into a normal KS4 topic.

CiLT

Some teachers are nervous about 'spoon-feeding' candidates by teaching them anything to do with writing that will subsequently lead to a piece of coursework. This is an over-interpretation of fair practice and it is not the intention of any of the exam boards that candidates should tackle a piece of coursework without having realistic preparation for that kind of writing. This means that the teacher may and should continue to **teach** up until the point students start to write the coursework in a connected, continuous form.

There are as many approaches to coursework as there are MFL teachers, but a typical approach is described briefly here, followed by more detailed guidance.

- Schedule a piece of coursework which fits well within the current teaching topic.

- Look carefully at the constituent parts of the content required. Include activities in a variety of skills which might subsequently provide candidates with useful ideas.

- Look carefully at the vocabulary or grammatical requirements that each piece of writing presents and rehearse relevant points (e.g. a particular tense) before starting the coursework.

- Provide the class with the title and any stimulus material and discuss the task with them. (This stage not always permissible.)

- Ask students to produce a plan or draft. (This stage not always permissible.)

- Provide an opportunity for students to write their final draft, in 'formal' controlled conditions (see page 21), in normal classwork conditions, or as independent homework.

- Afterwards, to maximise the potential for long-term improvement of writing, feed back to the whole class key points from your marking of this coursework assignment, with plenty of examples.

Make simple discourse markers such as 'but' and 'most importantly' an explicit teaching point – students do not learn these 'by osmosis' and they make a great difference to turning a selection of disjointed sentences into a piece of narrative writing. Also try to teach a selection of time references which allow a variety of tenses to be introduced. Look at the example overleaf of a writing task leading up to a piece of coursework on 'A haunted house'.

There are approx 90 words here but the many repititions mean that the mark for content will remain low

This is an attractive format which encouraged writing and enabled even the weakest candidate to produce simple descriptions

The teacher could help with further ideas: Why is the computer mysterious? What does it do?

Accuracy of articles is easily checked with a dictionary and they are also important if agreements are to be right

Dictionary could be used to improve accuracy

Agreements are vital in a piece of writing like this and more practice is clearly needed

Students had been taught *il y avait* but had no ideas for using it in this context, e.g. *Il y avait une grande piscine mais maintenant il n'y a que des arraignées dans la piscine*

This student could be encouraged to add more clauses like this

Teaching time references such as *autre temps* would improve further

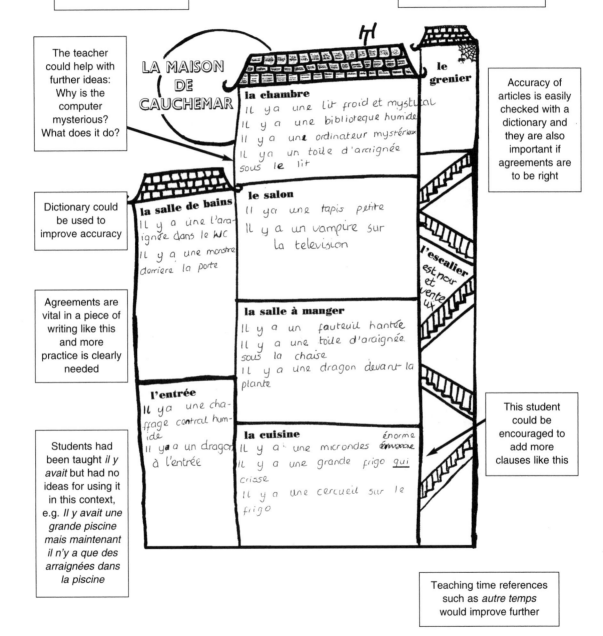

LA MAISON DE CAUCHEMAR

la chambre
Il y a une lit froid et mystical
Il y a une biblioteque humide
Il y a une ordinateur mystérieux
Il y a un toile d'araignée sous le lit

le grenier

la salle de bains
Il y a une l'araignée dans le WC
Il y a une monstre derriere la porte

le salon
Il y a une tapis petite
Il y a un vampire sur la television

l'escalier est noir et venteux

la salle à manger
Il y a un fauteuil hantée
Il y a une toile d'araignée sous la chaise
Il y a une dragon devant la plante

l'entrée
Il y a une chaffage central humide
Il y a a un dragon à l'entrée

la cuisine
Il y a une microndes énorme
Il y a une grande frigo qui crisse
Il y a une cercueil sur le frigo

CILT

HELPING STUDENTS TO PLAN EFFECTIVELY

Although boards are very strict about the amount of help a teacher may give once the students have started to write the coursework, all the boards encourage the teacher to assist at the planning stage (with the exception of OCR controlled-conditions tasks and WJEC). Students can be encouraged to produce a plan for their work and much of this planning work could be carried out as a whole class. It can also be helpful to provide a plan (in English or the target language) which guides students to include the kind of content necessary for maximising their marks (discussed from page 13 onwards). The following is an example of a supportive planning sheet for a simple 'critique' of a TV programme. It provides prompts in the target language without including 'chunks' of text which weaker candidates might merely copy.

GCSE Coursework 4

Critique d'une émission de télévision

Dessine un poster pour ton émission. Tu sais comment elle s'appelle en français?	Décris l'histoire (en trois phrases!).	Fais une liste des adjectifs qui décrivent cette émission.
Raconte quelque chose au sujet de cette émission – c'est quand? Elle dure combien de temps? C'est qu'elle sorte d'émission?	Devine ce qui va se passer dans la prochaine émission.	Phrases utiles.
Décris les vedettes.	Pourquoi aimes-tu cette émission? Et qu'est-ce que ta famille et tes amis en pensent?	

Note how the teacher has carefully anticipated the requirements for a range of tenses and opinions for candidates aiming for at least a grade C. She has also imposed a limit on the account of the plot, which is often the weakest feature of this kind of writing. However, the task starts with a short creative element, to 'get them going'. This sheet could be improved further by providing a clear opportunity to write in the past tense, although some candidates would include this in their account of the plot.

You might choose not to produce any plans for the content and structure of the coursework task, but you should still give careful thought to the kind of vocabulary and structure needed for success within each writing task. For example, 'A newspaper report of a fashion show' would need preparing in the following points:

- relevant vocabulary, e.g. clothes and descriptions;
- adjectival endings;
- relevant verbs in the past tense;
- comparatives;
- opinions;
- phrases such as 'is well known for'.

Brainstorming can be a useful activity here; for a piece of coursework on 'The school of the future' (AQA 'A' task 4b) you could brainstorm the relevant vocabulary and ideas of what to include. At this stage you could also check that students are secure with structures such as 'My school will be/will have …'. It is also important to remind them that to gain the highest marks they should seek to include opinions and references to the past, present and future in each piece of work. It is not enough for many candidates to be **told** this information, they need more concrete help in understanding what this implies for each piece of work. In a piece of coursework about 'The school of the future' it is easy to include opinion and references to the future (or conditional), but students may need help with ideas which allow them to refer to the past, e.g.:

'The primary school I went to was … so I would like a school which has …'.

Similarly in a piece of work on 'Me and my health', vary the tenses by writing about:

'What I ate last week and the exercise I took';

'Why I am always ill';

'My resolutions for the future'.

To cover a variety of tenses in a piece of writing about holidays you could teach students the relevant language for:

'Usually we go to …';

'Last year we went to …';

'Next year I would like to …'.

Give your students examples of how they could use language from a variety of topics in each context. For example, in 'The school of the future' candidates could include a description of a classroom, based on language used to describe their homes. Structure all coursework tasks so that they all include an opportunity to express attitudes and opinions (including justifications of opinions), or to analyse a situation.

DRAFTING

All boards (except WJEC) now permit candidates to draft their coursework (some have different drafting arrangements for controlled conditions pieces, so check page 41). Drafting and editing forms a major part of the teaching for our colleagues in the English department and is also considered best practice in most MFL teaching of writing. Students who are confident writers and are used to drafting then editing their own work will clearly benefit from producing a draft for their coursework, too. However, one colleague shows here that it might not always be the best way to approach coursework with all students:

> *'It's bad enough to get my lot sitting down and writing sensibly on one occasion!*
> *If I tried to get them to draft it first, they just wouldn't do it.'*

It is worth noting here that drafting is not actually compulsory. If you decide to go ahead with the drafting stage, all boards (except WJEC) now permit the use of a comments sheet (whose format is common to all the boards except SQA) to feedback to candidates on their draft (see your specification). You may not give any feedback, verbal or written, other than the comments sheet, and may only put a single tick in the relevant box (no other annotations permitted). Several colleagues who have tried using the comments sheet have not always found it successful – one otherwise diligent student felt victimised because the teacher had ticked almost every box. Another diligent student actually produced a final piece worse than the original because she changed every example of the features ticked, not just the 'incorrect' ones. Many of our weaker candidates just don't find this kind of relatively abstract feedback in this format helpful, although this may change as cohorts who have benefited from the National Literacy Strategy come into KS4. In fact, this feedback sheet might be more useful as a planning device for many candidates.

This means that you and your colleagues have to make some very careful decisions about the way of working which will suit **your** learners best. Some MFL teachers have already decided to use drafting as a teaching point throughout KS3 and 4, but to teach the relevant key vocabulary, structures and phrases for each coursework task and then to write it up without drafting, especially in controlled pieces.

> Centres should normally avoid providing a 'template' version of the coursework tasks where the basic structures have been chosen by the teacher and all that is left to candidates is to insert individual words and phrases. The only circumstances in which the use of a template is legitimate is when candidates are of a very low ability in speaking and writing and where such support is clearly acknowledged on the Candidate Record Form.
> *AQA 'B' GCSE Teacher Support Materials*

A related issue is how much support you choose to give at the planning stage of coursework. Shown here is an extract from a coursework support sheet drafted by a department which then showed it to me. My advice was to cut it into two halves! If the sheet was used as it is at the coursework stage, candidates are mainly copying and inserting words into gaps, so can be given very little credit for 'producing' the language. I suggested using the left-hand column as support at the planning/drafting stage of the piece of coursework and the right-hand side as a resource during the 'teaching' stage.

Mis vacaciones

¿Adónde fuiste de vacaciones el año pasado?	Fui a España/Italia/Grecia/Suiza/ los Estados Unidos.
¿Con quién fuiste?	Fui con mi familia/mis amigos/mis hermanos.
¿Cómo fuiste?	Fui en avión/en barco/en coche.
¿Qué tiempo hizo?	Hizo sol/calor/buen tempo/mal tempo.
¿Qué hiciste allí?	Tomé el sol/nadé en el mar/comí muchísmo/ salí con mis amigos.

USING DICTIONARIES IN COURSEWORK

The issue of dictionary skills is particularly tricky now that students will no longer be using dictionaries in the terminal exams. The QCA scheme of work for KS3 encourages the teaching of dictionary skills as an essential part of language apprenticeship, but you might be tempted to restrict the amount of time devoted to this. If so, and your learners are not fully proficient with their use, you might prefer to 'ban' the use of dictionaries in coursework completely. If you do so, remember to make a note of this in the information about the coursework sent to your moderator (see page 27 onwards on moderation).

As coursework is written under less stressful, 'more natural' conditions, it is reasonable for exam boards to expect a higher standard of writing than has been the case in terminal exam writing papers. In particular, as candidates have access to dictionaries, even under controlled conditions, there will be no excuse for poor spelling, wrong articles and missing words. However, a dictionary in untrained hands is a dangerous weapon and unless you teach dictionary skills, you might be faced with pages of mis-translation such as:

'En hiver, tu puissance abeille pouvoir carrure un neige homme'

(In winter you might be able to build a snowman!)

One approach to effective use of dictionaries in coursework is to tell students at the planning stage to look up all the vocabulary they are likely to need. This means that you have an opportunity to check for potential 'howlers' at this stage. During the actual writing stage, encourage students to use dictionaries mostly to improve the accuracy of their work by checking such things as spellings, articles and correct prepositions with verbs. For further guidance see Pathfinder 28: *Making effective use of the dictionary* (see references).

Maximising attainment in coursework

It is important to give students ideas for their writing at the planning stage so that they can maximise the content. Some boards limit the amount of other marks that can be awarded, according to the number of marks awarded for content. The word count can also affect the number of marks that can be awarded for coursework, so encourage all candidates to aim for at least 100 words in each piece of writing. Explain to them that the board's suggested numbers of words are minimums. When checking students' plans before writing, try to anticipate their problems and advise them on these before they start to write.

This worksheet is taken from *Write on … writing skills for GCSE coursework* (Tyson-Ward 2001) and although it looks simple, serves several very important purposes:

- it provides students with a 'framework' for their writing which doesn't deny them credit for any of the language produced (research shows that unconfident writers are put off by a 'blank piece of paper');

- it prevents students devoting too much time to drawing or illustrating their work;

- it provides a rough structure for the task – describe your current uniform first, then say what you would prefer to wear;

- it provides opportunities for contrastive writing (i.e. comparing uniform and preferred clothing) which are likely to be complex opinions e.g. 'My school uniform is too hot in summer because we have to wear a blazer, but girls aren't allowed to wear trousers so it's too cold in winter. So I would prefer to wear something that is …';

- inclusion of sports equipment in the illustrations reminds candidates that they can bring in relevant content from other areas to expand their writing.

Source: Tyson-Ward S Write on … writing skills for GCSE coursework (© MLG Publishing)

It might help you and your colleagues to both plan and mark coursework by looking at the following table. It is a summary of the key points expected at each level across all of the exam boards.

CiLT

Grades A*/A/B	Detailed description or accounts
	Variety of expressions of opinion with justifications
	Simple analysis (where appropriate), e.g. compares cultural features
	Coherent structure to text
	Use of three tenses
	Range of vocabulary and some use of idiom
	Subordinate clauses/complex verbal constructions
	Sentences linked in a variety of ways
	Generally accurate spelling or grammar
	Complex structures attempted (but not always successfully)
Grades C/D	Continuous writing with some simple linking
	Regularly goes beyond a minimum response
	Mainly narrative or descriptive
	Opinions included
	At least two tenses
	More accurate than inaccurate in spelling and grammar
	Includes more than one 'person'
Grades E/F/G	A minimal response
	Some verb usage
	Might be repetitive and/or supported
	Sentences might not be linked or arranged in a logical order
	Could include copying phrases or adapting a model

PROVIDING IDEAS FOR WRITING TASKS

Students are more likely to produce coursework full of relevant content if they have interesting writing tasks. It is difficult to link cause and effect here, but one of the features I regularly see is that the departments who score well in coursework tend to be more adventurous in their choice of coursework tasks. Planning for coursework may give your department an opportunity to look for stimulating materials for Key Stage 4 and find topics which will actually make students want to write. This piece of coursework comes from Rebecca Munslow who teaches at St Paul's School for Girls, Edgbaston. She chose to tackle the topics of leisure activities and young people today in a comparison with young people under the Nazi regime. First of all, she revised relevant vocabulary and expanded it further in both present and past tenses. She then showed the class photographs of the 'German Girls' League' and 'Hitler Youth' and asked students to describe what the young people were doing. As homework, students were asked to read background materials on these two organisations in English and some were given the option to research their own reading materials on the Internet. Students then had to respond to simple comprehension tasks such as 'Which of these activities do you do?', 'Which activities would you not like to do?'. After further reading and listening tasks, students were given a four-stage plan for the coursework:

- Introduction – 'I'm going to write about … because …';
- describe the kinds of activities the Bund Deutscher Mädel and/or Hitler Jugend did;
- compare with activities you do nowadays;
- Conclusion – 'I think/In my opinion … are similar/different'.

In addition, students were given a vocabulary sheet with less familiar items such as 'marching', 'flags' and 'lessons in political ideology'!

Vergleiche das Leben von jungen Leuten in Nazi Deutschland und heute

Ich werde über Jungen und Mädchen in Nazi Deutschland schreiben.

Use of future tense in the first sentence

Good use of perfect and imperfect tenses in an accessible context

In Nazi Deutschland haben die meisten Mädchen an dem Bund Deutscher Mädel angehört. In den Lagern haben sie Volkslieder gesungen. Sie haben auch gebastelt und sie haben Sport getrieben, wie Gymnastik und Aerobik. Sie haben auch Antreten und Marschieren geübt. Die Mädchen wurden politisch geschult. Sie haben nützliche Fächer gelernt wie Kochen und Krankenpflege.

Teacher support given for unusual vocabulary

This is similar to describing a school uniform, a topic most candidates are confident with

Die Mädchen hatten auch eine Uniform, sie bestand aus einem dunkelblauen Rock, eine weiße Bluse und einem Tuch, schwarz mit einem Lederknoten.

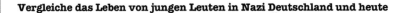

Judicious use of illustration – enough to show differences

Heute gehen die jungen Leute Windsurfen und Schwimmen. Heute kann man Stadtbummel machen oder ins Kino gehen jede Woche. Deutschlands Jugend ist sehr aktiv und verbringt wenig Zeit zu Hause. Im Gegensatz zu vor fünfzig Jahren junge Leute heute haben viele Freizeit. Nach der Schule treffen die junge Leute ihre Freunde und gehen aus.

Standard 'freetime and hobbies' vocabulary

A complex opinion with an interesting discourse marker

Meiner Meinung nach war Nazi Deutschland sehr verschieden. Heute hingegen Jugend kann machen was sie wollen.

Summary opinion – good cultural comparison

(160 words)

CiLT

This has led to the production of genuinely interesting and worthwhile pieces of writing which score well in the coursework context. Note how much of the content is 'standard' GCSE level vocabulary about leisure activities which has been placed into a more sophisticated (and intellectually stimulating) context. Similarly, look for cross-curricular issues which may give the students a strong opportunity to write by making use of research they have already done in another subject. For example, students taking art may be studying the lives of a famous artist and could write a biography or a description of the artist's work for coursework.

CHOOSING YOUR COURSEWORK TASKS

An initial reading of many of the GCSE specifications seems to imply that candidates choose when and how to do coursework and select the task themselves. This is clearly unrealistic for all but the most able and trustworthy 'self-starter' although this modus operandi might be familiar to colleagues in other GCSE subjects, or even in AS/A level languages. A far more typical approach to coursework in GCSE MFLs would be for the teacher to decide the timing, title and exact approach to each piece of coursework. In some other subjects it is considered best practice to maximise student choice, and indeed even with coursework firmly managed by the class teacher (or even the MFL department as a whole) there is still room for some personalisation – candidates can write about their own holiday or work experience, they can select the famous person or favourite leisure activity and so on.

Even if you have chosen a GCSE specification which gives you a bank of tasks for coursework, it is still worth spending some time considering which tasks fit best into your departmental scheme of work. When planning or choosing your coursework tasks, include plenty of examples of the types of tasks your students are best at, for example, biographies, narrative writing and interviews. Take special care with trickier tasks such as 'planning a holiday' (rather than an account of a holiday) as they might be writing in a tense they are not used to within this topic.

Edexcel's requirements mean that a 'unit' of coursework can be composed of several shorter pieces of writing, but the nature of the tasks set by AQA and WJEC would make this approach more difficult.

Choosing your coursework tasks

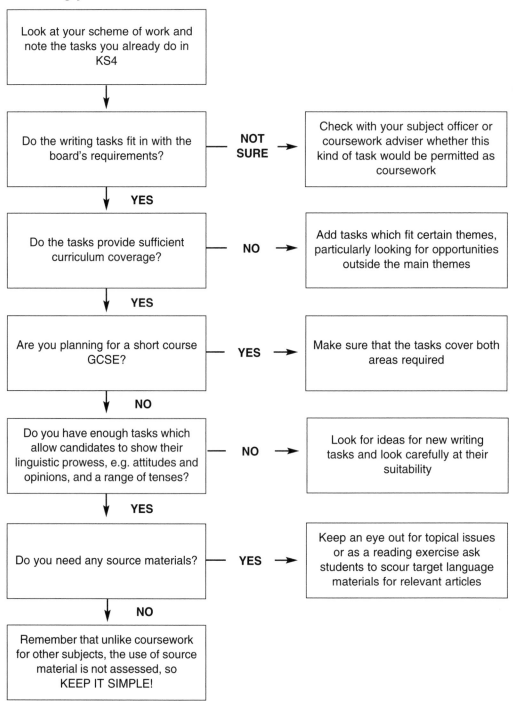

CiLT

Here is an example of how coursework allows for a wider range of topics than can be used in a terminal examination. Travel and transport is a topic area which can be difficult to exploit as a piece of writing, but careful planning has allowed this candidate to produce a piece of coursework on an area which interests him.

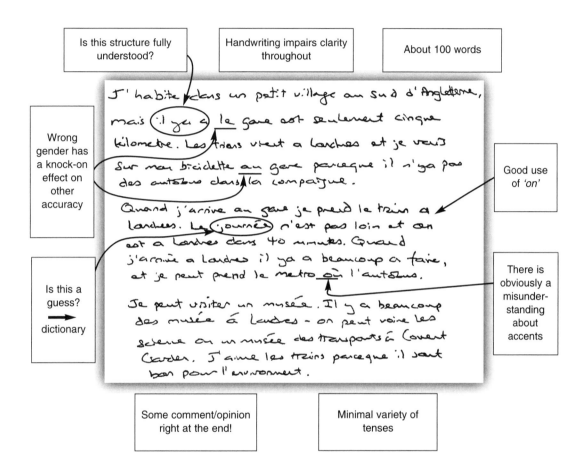

Is this structure fully understood?

Handwriting impairs clarity throughout

About 100 words

Wrong gender has a knock-on effect on other accuracy

Good use of 'on'

Is this a guess?
→
dictionary

There is obviously a misunderstanding about accents

Some comment/opinion right at the end!

Minimal variety of tenses

3. Meeting the exam board's requirements

Some language teachers might have been deterred from adopting the coursework option so far as they are intimidated by the exam board's requirements for conducting coursework. Among the questions asked are: 'What does "controlled conditions" mean?', 'What do I do if they cheat?', 'How much help are they allowed?'. Teachers should recognise the many years' experience we already have in conducting various kinds of assessment including GAML, GNVQ and regular in-class assessment as well as the requirements of conducting – or even assessing – the orals. However, it might be helpful for you and your colleagues to consider what constitutes unfair practice in the coursework situation. A sensible 'rule of thumb' to apply is to decide whether something would be considered as 'cheating' in a terminal exam. Read the following six questions and decide on a yes/no answer for each one.

IS THAT CHEATING?

1. The student has written a piece of coursework at home and it clearly looks as though he or she has had substantial amounts of help.

   Yes, it is cheating! In an examination situation students would not be permitted to have help from another person, so it is easy to see that the same would apply when doing coursework.

   > The use of resources does not extend to humans.
   > *OCR GCSE Specification*

2. The class teacher has helped the student to write the coursework.

   The nature of support the teacher is permitted to give differs from one board to another. You have to be clear what amounts of teacher intervention your board permits (see pages 24 and 41).

3. The student has copied a piece of writing from a published source.

   Yes, this is cheating! This is plagiarism, but if students are writing a piece of work which requires source materials such as brochures, websites and newspaper cuttings (less likely at GCSE level), make sure that they understand that they should not copy. Some boards require that all source materials used are listed in the paperwork for each piece of coursework.

4. The student has learnt a good piece of their own writing off by heart and reproduces it under controlled conditions.

This is what many of us have been doing for years to prepare students for writing in the terminal examinations! While it does not represent a sophisticated level of learning, it would be permissible in an examination situation. However, it is not within the spirit of coursework and we discuss this more fully in Chapter 2.

5. The student has used a sample letter at the back of a dictionary and adapted it appropriately to the task set.

   This is similar to the way in which many bilingual secretaries are trained. Use of dictionaries is permitted by all the boards for writing coursework. However, students need to be aware that they should not merely copy and they need to fulfil the brief of the task. See also page 11 on use of templates.

6. The student has used grammar tables at the back of a dictionary or mnemonics on the classroom walls to improve the accuracy of his or her writing.

   This student is a more sophisticated language learner than the ones imagined in points 4 and 5! As long as the student is not copying disembodied chunks of language, this practice should be positively encouraged!

CONTROLLED CONDITIONS

Doing a minimum amount of coursework under controlled conditions allows the marker, the standardising team and the moderator to have maximum information about one element of the coursework portfolio, in the same way that the viva voce acts as the 'controlled-conditions' element of the PhD. If you are entering candidates for WJEC or Scottish Standard Grades, then all your coursework must be carried out under controlled conditions (so discussions of alternatives in this chapter do not apply). While working under more open conditions might suit learning and teaching in other GCSE subjects, doing all your coursework under controlled conditions – or just in the classroom – is probably the easiest way to manage the coursework process in MFL in order to avoid malpractice.

Controlled conditions provide an effective way of verifying coursework authenticity.
Edexcel GCSE Coursework Guide

The purpose of the controlled conditions assignment is to provide 'benchmarked' assessment information to compare with assessments for assignments produced under non-controlled conditions.
AQA 'A' Teachers' Guide

As Modern Language teachers we are already accustomed to carrying out our own periodic assessments inside the classroom – working under 'controlled conditions' is not dissimilar to this. Writing coursework under controlled conditions can include working in the normal classroom during lesson time, provided that the class teacher can be sure that the work is a student's own and not the result of a joint effort.

At least one third of the coursework submission must be done under controlled conditions ... Work must be done in the classroom and supervised by the teacher.
Edexcel GCSE Coursework Guide

The surroundings are less stressful and candidates are, within given parameters, able to treat them as a normal part of class work. ... Candidates will not be allowed to collaborate, but otherwise normal classroom conditions should prevail.
WJEC Coursework Guidelines

Coursework carried out under controlled conditions must be completed under the supervision of a teacher and with all candidates meeting together at the same time, probably in the same room. The atmosphere should be formal and no communication is allowed between candidates. There is no stipulation of a time limit.
OCR GCSE Specification

'The final submissions [after drafting] must ... be written in class, within 30 minutes, under supervision, with no support or recourse to notes or reference sources other than a dictionary.'
SQA National Qualifications – Standard Grade Modern Languages

It may be a good idea to complete the first few pieces of work under controlled conditions, until students understand what is required of them in Modern Languages coursework. The class teacher needs to ensure that students are using only permitted support, such as dictionaries, and that there are no factors which will unduly enhance or impair a candidate's performance. It is important to do more than the minimum required number of pieces of coursework under controlled conditions to give you the largest possible range of coursework to choose from to submit to the board. Many teachers have decided to carry out all their coursework in the classroom, though not necessarily under the strictest 'controlled' conditions.

Teachers are free to hold as many sessions of controlled coursework as they wish. If they prefer or have any doubts about the amount of help received for independent work, they can select, for final submission, more than one item completed under controlled conditions.
OCR GCSE Specification

While it is important not to sacrifice too much valuable and scarce contact time with students for doing coursework under controlled conditions, it can be difficult to get some students to write outside of the classroom. If that is the case, students could write all of their coursework in controlled conditions, using the one or two homework slots leading up to this for planning and collecting information. End-of-year exams and 'mocks' can be used to provide time for controlled-conditions coursework.

TEACHER INTERVENTION

It is important that you agree as a department or centre what kind of support you are going to give, and to communicate these requirements clearly to students. Each exam board permits a different level of intervention by the class teacher.

AQA A and B	Although teachers will discuss coursework assignments in advance with candidates, they must not comment on or correct any language produced by the candidate once he or she has begun to draft the work to be submitted, other than by using the Comments Sheet.
Edexcel	It is perfectly acceptable to give a student advice on the content of a piece of work, to suggest expansion of a certain section or the introduction of more description or opinion. General advice can also be given on the linguistic content, but specific errors must not be indicated.
OCR	The teacher is allowed to comment on one draft only (but not at all in controlled-conditions work). The teacher must be very careful about the extent to which he or she intervenes in the process. Verbal or written detailed interventions belong to the task-training phase.
WJEC	Teachers are not allowed to assist students apart from in distributing materials needed for the completion of tasks set.
Scotland	Candidates may consult notes, written texts and reference sources to draft their pieces of writing, and they should be encouraged to redraft following advice from the teacher.

Managing the coursework – Some reminders

Setting and monitoring the task

- If students are going to write different tasks (e.g. a 'famous person' of their own choosing), agree a title with each student and note this agreed title in writing – some boards provide 'frontsheets' which fulfil this function. If you are not sure whether it is a suitable piece of writing for coursework, check this with the exam board at this point.

- Make sure that students understand what the requirements of the coursework task are. If the task is 'Advertising your local area' it is not acceptable if students decide to write about their house instead of their town.

- Keep the time permitted for submitting each piece of coursework short; students may begin to forget the relevant language for a particular topic if they leave it too long before writing about it.

- Set coursework tasks regularly throughout Years 10 and 11, and plan for more than the three (five for WJEC) minimum required pieces of coursework. It is important that the last coursework deadline is well in advance of the date required by the exam board to allow time for marking, standardisation and selection of the portfolio.

Presentation of coursework

On most markschemes presentation does not gain marks but candidates must be aware of the need for clarity. Unlike coursework in many other GCSE subjects, there is no credit awarded for inclusion of pictures, graphs, maps, illustrations and title pages. However, labelling pictures and diagrams can be a good way for lower-ability candidates to increase their word count, but to prevent students investing too much time and effort in collecting pictures rather than writing in the target language it can be helpful to have a 'rule' requiring all illustrations to be labelled in the target language.

There is no premium for the use of ICT when writing coursework, but all work should be legible. Many MFL teachers agree that many candidates write **less** accurately when they word-process, often because they do not know where to find accents. On the other hand, ICT can be an important motivational factor in writing in a foreign language, so its use might be encouraged – students can use ICT to write their coursework outside the classroom, e.g. in the library, as long as this is not a piece of controlled-conditions coursework. Most boards (see page 41) permit the use of ICT under controlled conditions as long as all the other requirements are met. All ICT use must be declared, including details of software, therefore the use of translation software is likely to severely limit the marks awarded and its use should be prevented.

If you suspect that your candidates have been using translation software without declaring it (which constitutes malpractice) look for the following features: register of vocabulary in excess of usual standard, e.g. idiom; literal translations e.g. T- shirt = *thé chemise*, walking boots = *gehende Stiefel*; any misspelled English words will not be recognised by the software so will be retained in the final piece.

The following piece of coursework shows some important features of the presentation of coursework.

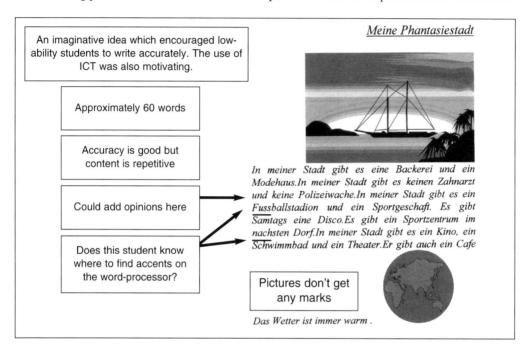

As it is possible that you will be doing most of your coursework in class time, it is unlikely that the issues arising in coursework for other subjects will be a major problem – i.e. candidates not observing deadlines. However, it is still important to recognise the importance of careful storage of the coursework and all the information about marks awarded, source/stimulus materials and conditions under which the coursework was completed.

Boards require various frontsheets and supplementary information to be added to the coursework, usually including a declaration from the candidates themselves that this is their own work. It is a good idea to complete such paperwork 'as you go' to avoid an end-of-year rush. Here is an example of a record sheet for the department's own use which has been designed so that students can fill in the top half themselves.

COLLECTING THE COURSEWORK

COURSEWORK RECORD SHEET					
Name					
Class					
Assignment title	1			2	
Word count					
Controlled conditions: Yes/No					
Source materials used and software (e.g. course book, dictionary)					
For teachers' use					
Theme/Topic/Area/ Assignment code					
Tenses covered					
Attitudes and opinions					
Teacher's mark	/8	/6	/6		/8
Standardised mark	/8	/6	/6		/8
Comments					

Marking, standardisation and moderation

Marking the coursework

Many language teachers believe that coursework is driving up the standard of written work. This could well be true as students can now prepare for the writing task and use reference materials throughout. This means that when we are marking coursework, we should set high expectations of both technical accuracy and content. Each board has produced clear grade descriptions/criteria for each category of marks which should be applied in the same way as the National Curriculum levels, i.e. by finding the 'best fit' level for the piece of work. The grid in the appendix (page 41) gives a summary of each board's markscheme, but you should look at the specification and any additional guidance issued by your board. It is particularly important to note that the word count and quality of content effectively limit the range of marks which can be awarded for the other areas such as accuracy and quality of language. This rule has been introduced to avoid a situation whereby students could get full marks for accuracy by keeping their work just a few words long! However, it is worth explaining to students that they should not write too much if this is at the expense of accuracy and good use of language.

Students will benefit greatly if they understand the markscheme and if their earlier writing is marked according to the board's criteria and returned to students liberally annotated.

Task training

The teacher may decide, especially during the earlier stages of the course, to allow the candidates to work through a task in detail as part of the process of training and practice. For such a practice task, the teacher could comment, intervene and correct as with any piece of written class work. However, such a piece **cannot** be submitted as a coursework task. Any subsequent coursework task submitted for GCSE **must not** be identical with or closely resemble a practice task.

OCR GCSE Specification

If any candidates qualify for special consideration, the board should be informed early – your exams officer will know about the appropriate procedures. This could include candidates unable to complete the required number of pieces because of absence. If you have a candidate who has changed schools during Years 10 or 11, it is often possible to accept coursework done at the other centre. However, exact arrangements in such cases depend on the point at which this happens during KS4, so again, you should seek guidance from your examinations officer and board.

Losing coursework

The blunt advice here is – don't! Coursework should be kept securely once candidates have submitted it. Bitter experience and common sense show that it is not appropriate to rely on students to store their own portfolios. Should, for any reason, coursework become lost or otherwise unavailable (e.g. flood damage), ask your examinations officer to follow the board's procedures for this eventuality.

STANDARDISATION

It is important to understand that boards moderate only a sample of the coursework from your whole centre and therefore moderators make the assumption that all teachers within that centre are marking to the same standard. Standardisation is a compulsory part of coursework and there could be serious repercussions for centres who do not standardise effectively. If you have to standardise the **marking** of a piece of coursework as a language team, this logically implies that you should collaborate as a team in the **planning** of each piece of work.

> It is important for all teachers whose students are going to do coursework to plan jointly. This will enable teachers to pool ideas and will lead to a feeling of greater confidence ... This will make the process of standardising marking within the department simpler and more efficient.
> *Edexcel GCSE Coursework Guide*

Many departments have found that the discussions before, during and after coursework have actually enhanced practice within their department:

> *'Standardisation as a department has been really good for joint planning, because after the first year we saw what other teachers did and we've come up with a bigger list of possibilities or ideas ... It's helped with preparation. It's helped with ideas, so it's got us together a bit more.'* (Adams 2000: 20)

The exam boards demand that work is standardised within each centre. A simple way to organise this is to copy some examples of students' coursework which each member of the department (or all teachers of that language) mark individually according to the board's criteria. The marks are compared and an interpretation of the markscheme is agreed. It can save time to do this standardisation process before large quantities of coursework have been marked so that marks are less likely to have to be adjusted.

Heads of Department should be assertive about asking headteachers for INSET and non-contact time for standardisation – colleagues from other subjects have had such resources made available to them for several years!

Ideally, you should not apply the board's assessment criteria either too leniently or too strictly. Of vital importance, however, is that assessment is consistent across all of the teachers of each language in the department. As long as work is consistently marked, the board's moderator can adjust marks if necessary. It is important to understand that if one of your team is a 'rogue' marker, it might cause the results of **all** your candidates to be moderated downwards!

If you have exceptionally talented candidates (for example, students bilingual in the language being examined) you should not penalise the work of your other Grade A and A* candidates just because their work is not of the same standard – remember that coursework is criterion-referenced and not norm-referenced. You should also take care that you are not marking more severely in one language compared to the others taught in your department. This is particularly the case in a highly inflected language such as German, where there is simply a greater range of potential errors for the average candidate to choose from! If you are the only teacher of a particular language in the department, it can be helpful to work with a teacher of that language from a nearby school, but this is not obligatory.

MODERATION AND SAMPLING

Moderation is the process whereby the exam board looks at a sample of your marking to judge whether the marking criteria have been correctly applied. After receiving the coursework marks, the board will usually inform centres which candidates' work it would like to see for moderation. It is important to keep **all** coursework until the October/November after the exam and it may also be helpful to keep exemplar work from the previous year to help in departmental planning. Centres can appeal against coursework decisions in the same way they can appeal against other GCSE assessment decisions, but to do this they must have securely retained the coursework of all candidates.

Moderators usually select their samples by taking a representative sample from across the mark range. They will assume that the school – even if marking too leniently or severely – has judged the rank order correctly. This means it is important for the centre to check its rank order. One way to do this is to take samples of pieces of work from different teachers with close but differing marks and to see if the implied rank order can be justified by comparing these candidates' work. (Similarly take work with the same marks and see if the award can be justified.)

Some boards ask centres to provide extra information about the circumstances under which the coursework was prepared and produced for the moderator. Edexcel and OCR, for example, ask centres to submit all stimulus materials, while in AQA 'A' Linear this is optional but strongly encouraged. This is your opportunity to let the moderator know whether your candidates have worked independently and therefore you have given generous credit for what they have produced, or that they were given a great deal of support (such as templates and writing frames discussed on page 13) which is reflected in your less generous marking (look at again at the 'wedge' diagram on page 6).

Comments are especially necessary if marks awarded are higher or lower than the assessment criteria suggest or if the candidate has received help other than the assistance laid down as allowable.
OCR GCSE Specification

Whatever support you have given at the coursework stage, it is not a requirement by any of the boards that you submit every worksheet and classroom task you have done while teaching the unit! The exam board's moderator (not to mention OFSTED and your headteacher!) will assume that you will have thoroughly taught the relevant language unit in all four skills before embarking on the coursework.

4. Exam board requirements: what students need to know!

One of the difficulties that KS4 students experience in studying languages effectively is that they do not fully understand what is expected of them during Years 10 and 11. One of the advantages of coursework is that it helps to provide a structure for the whole GCSE programme. Specifications don't always provide the kind of information that students need to help them understand the time-scale and workload. It might therefore be helpful to use a planner for the five-term period of the GCSE course like the one below. It is important that this planner also gives an indication of any other obligations or events that take place in Years 10 and 11. This helps to show students that it is important to keep up to date with their Modern Languages work, as well as coursework from other subjects.

Modern Languages coursework planner

Month	Year 10	Month	Year 11
Sept		Sept	
Oct	Writing coursework 1: Profile of a famous person (controlled conditions)	Oct	Writing coursework 4: My work experience (controlled conditions)
Nov		Nov	
Dec		Dec	Year 11 Mock GCSEs – Writing coursework 5: Letter to a problem page
Jan	Writing coursework 2: A special occasion (controlled conditions)	Jan	
Feb		Feb	Writing coursework 6 (optional)
Mar	Exchange visit to France	Mar	Preparation of speaking presentation
Apr		Apr	Orals start
May	Year 10 exams – Writing coursework 3: My holiday or exchange (controlled conditions)	May	Study leave
Jun	Work experience	Jun	Reading and Listening exams
Jul	Exchange partners arrive	Jul	

If students are to complete coursework successfully, they need to have a clear idea about the board's expectations and especially how these differ from coursework in other subjects. Boards ask teachers to remind candidates regularly about unfair practices.

> At the start of the course the supervising teacher is responsible for informing candidates of the regulations concerning malpractice. Candidates must not take part in any unfair practice and must understand that to present materials copied directly from books or other sources without acknowledgement will be regarded as deliberate deception.
> *AQA 'A' Specification*

In addition to explaining coursework procedures, it is worth telling students how coursework is marked. For example, if your board is AQA you could explain that marks available for Quality of Language are limited by the success of the Communication (i.e. the content). The criteria for the award of the different grade bands (such as inclusion of a variety of tenses) are clearly defined in the QCA criteria so these can also be summarised for students:

What kind of writing is expected for the different grades?

Grades G, F, E
- an ability to write individual words, short sentences and set phrases
- communicate the main points of the message or task

Grades D, C
- an ability to write linked sentences
- use a range of tenses
- express personal opinions
- write simple formal and informal letters

Grades B, A, A*
- an ability to use longer sequences of language
- give factual information
- express and justify ideas and points of view
- use a range of tenses, structures and vocabulary
- produce writing where the grammar and spelling are accurate
- write in an appropriate style

One common problem is that students don't take MFL coursework seriously – ironically one of the reasons for this can be because our coursework assignments are so short. We have already discussed the advantages of controlled conditions, and using an A4 proforma like the one overleaf can reinforce the status of this work as a piece of exam assessment.

GCSE SPANISH COURSEWORK

Name	Candidate number

School	Centre number

Date	Target length 150–200 words

Title *A day that went wrong*

_____

_____

_____

_____

_____

5. Key Stage 3 and 'coursework'

Coursework can form the basis of written work in KS3, building up to a portfolio. All you need for a portfolio is lined paper and treasury tags! Pupils can design their own title page and compile a contents page as they go along. Not only does 'coursework' in KS3 help to prepare the ground for examined work in Years 10 and 11, but also good practice in writing is established early. Research shows that work for maximising attainment in the GCSE must begin in KS3 because it is too late by KS4!

Pupils are introduced to effective drafting processes in KS2 as part of the NLS, so adapt these processes for use in the MFL classroom. Encourage them to proof-read and redraft their work by making these activities (a) a fun activity and ultimately (b) an accepted practice in the classroom routine. (See Pathfinder 40: *Just write!* pages 33–39 for further ideas in this area.)

Make liberal use of various kinds of support for writing in the MFL classroom so that when these pupils 'graduate' into KS4 they should be able to write without undue support. Writing frames are particularly helpful at this stage, where the relationship between the amount of teacher support and pupil input is not so crucial. The writing frame overleaf shows how KS3 candidates can be supported to write about interesting topics even with modest amounts of language. These approaches reflect the best practice recommended in the KS3 National Strategy for MFL. In particular, the objectives in the routes focusing on Word-, Sentence- and Text-level work are most likely to be able to help pupils progress in writing.

- Encourage redrafting of written work – follow the example of colleagues in the English department and ensure that drafts are completed in exercise books, rather than on disposable pieces of paper.

- Highlight errors in initial drafts and provide appropriate support to rectify these in the final draft; for example, dictionaries to correct spelling errors and grammar summaries relevant to the topic being studied.

- Develop writing in other areas of language work such as regular self-assessment and profiling, or keeping a reading diary (see Pathfinder 36: *More reading for pleasure in a foreign language).*

- Build preparation for written work into your regular drilling – graded questions are equally useful for reading and writing.

- Be realistic about the amount of support that pupils need when they write in a foreign language.

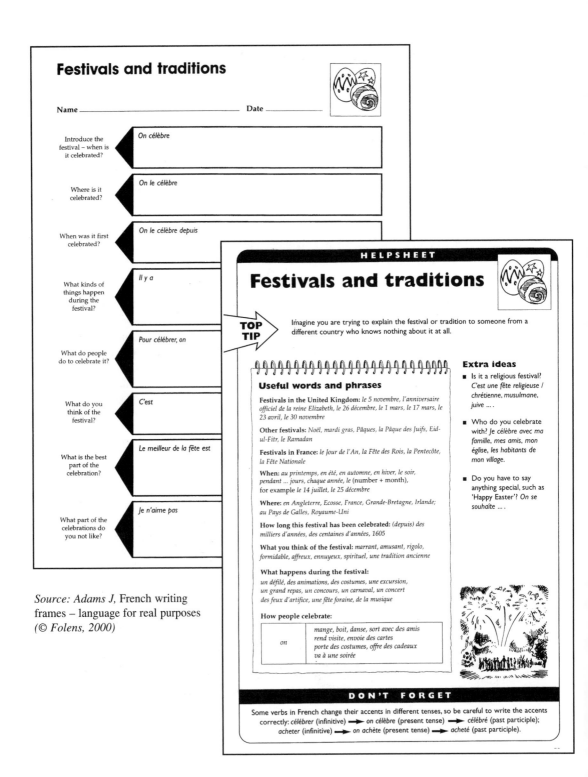

Festivals and traditions

Name _____ Date _____

Introduce the festival – when is it celebrated?	On célèbre
Where is it celebrated?	On le célèbre
When was it first celebrated?	On le célèbre depuis
What kinds of things happen during the festival?	Il y a
What do people do to celebrate it?	Pour célébrer, on
What do you think of the festival?	C'est
What is the best part of the celebration?	Le meilleur de la fête est
What part of the celebrations do you not like?	Je n'aime pas

Source: Adams J, French writing frames – language for real purposes *(© Folens, 2000)*

HELPSHEET

Festivals and traditions

TOP TIP → Imagine you are trying to explain the festival or tradition to someone from a different country who knows nothing about it at all.

Useful words and phrases

Festivals in the United Kingdom: *le 5 novembre, l'anniversaire officiel de la reine Elizabeth, le 26 décembre, le 1 mars, le 17 mars, le 23 avril, le 30 novembre*

Other festivals: *Noël, mardi gras, Pâques, la Pâque des Juifs, Eid-ul-Fitr, le Ramadan*

Festivals in France: *le Jour de l'An, la Fête des Rois, la Pentecôte, la Fête Nationale*

When: *au printemps, en été, en automne, en hiver, le soir, pendant ... jours, chaque année, le (number + month), for example le 14 juillet, le 25 décembre*

Where: *en Angleterre, Ecosse, France, Grande-Bretagne, Irlande; au Pays de Galles, Royaume-Uni*

How long this festival has been celebrated: *(depuis) des milliers d'années, des centaines d'années, 1605*

What you think of the festival: *marrant, amusant, rigolo, formidable, affreux, ennuyeux, spirituel, une tradition ancienne*

What happens during the festival: *un défilé, des animations, des costumes, une excursion, un grand repas, un concours, un carnaval, un concert des feux d'artifice, une fête foraine, de la musique*

How people celebrate:

| on | *mange, boit, danse, sort avec des amis rend visite, envoie des cartes porte des costumes, offre des cadeaux va à une soirée* |

Extra ideas

- Is it a religious festival? *C'est une fête religieuse / chrétienne, musulmane, juive ... .*

- Who do you celebrate with? *Je célèbre avec ma famille, mes amis, mon église, les habitants de mon village.*

- Do you have to say anything special, such as 'Happy Easter'? *On se souhaite ... .*

DON'T FORGET

Some verbs in French change their accents in different tenses, so be careful to write the accents correctly: *célébrer* (infinitive) → *on célèbre* (present tense) → *célébré* (past participle); *acheter* (infinitive) → *on achète* (present tense) → *acheté* (past participle).

CILT

WHY COLLECT A PORTFOLIO OF WRITTEN TASKS IN KS3?

- Pupils can see clearly for themselves that their range of skills and topics in the target language is progressing – in learning a language there is much work which doesn't have a 'visible' outcome, such as listening tasks.

- Portfolios can be used to show to parents, to display at open evenings, or to add to the pupil's record of achievement.

- Good pieces of writing can be entered for language competitions such as MLG's 'Free Spirit' poetry and song competition (for more details contact at002@netgates.co.uk).

The following piece of 'project work' from Year 8 shows clearly how KS3 writing differs from successful GCSE coursework.

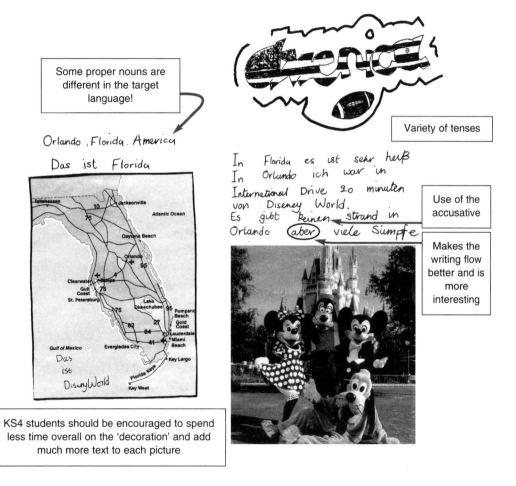

Some proper nouns are different in the target language!

Variety of tenses

Use of the accusative

Makes the writing flow better and is more interesting

KS4 students should be encouraged to spend less time overall on the 'decoration' and add much more text to each picture

6. Coursework and bilingual learners

One of the frustrations experienced by most learners in a foreign language is that the sophistication of their message often far outstrips their linguistic ability to communicate that message. Bilingual learners using their mother tongue, community language or heritage language can differ from this pattern in that they are likely to communicate fluently but have other learning needs such as the development of accuracy. This is particularly true of some bilinguals who can be strong in listening and speaking, but might never have formally learnt to read and write in their heritage language. Such learners might not even fully understand that the standard of their written work falls behind that of their spoken skills. They may therefore benefit from drilling practice of grammar points.

One of the main advantages that bilingual learners have is their contact with the target language culture. You can allow them to exploit this knowledge and wide vocabulary to its fullest extent by careful choice of coursework tasks. Any task which brings in the target language country is advantageous, especially if candidates can also compare it with the relevant feature of life in the UK:

* an account of a visit to the target language country;
* a special occasion;
* comparison of media in the UK and abroad;
* a social or environmental issue in the target language community.

The following piece of Urdu coursework about work experience was written by a middle-achieving student at the end of Year 10. It displays many of the characteristics of a bilingual user of any language in that there is good depth of meaning and interesting content, but some problems with the accuracy of endings – especially those which are silent – informal register, regional language use and transference errors from English.

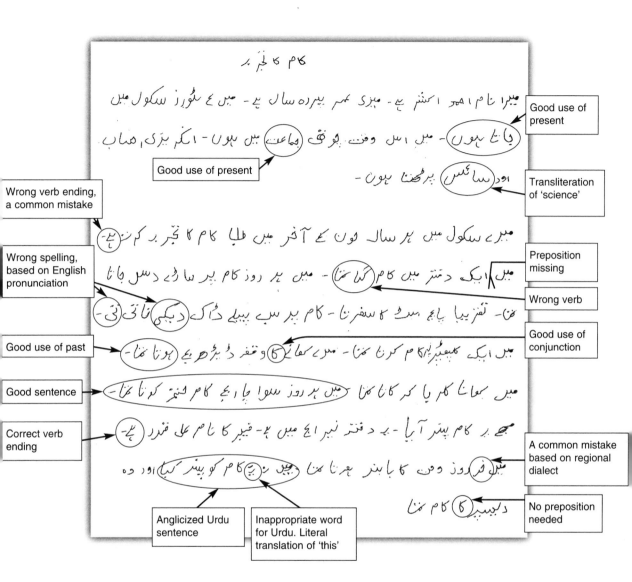

7. Troubleshooting – What do I do if …?

What do I do if a student does a dreadful piece of coursework?

Get them to write another one! All the boards permit candidates to write more than the minimum pieces required, and you should allow for this in planning your scheme of work. This then permits you to select the best pieces of work for each candidate to submit to the board.

What can I do if the student has consistently under-performed in coursework?

You can enter the candidate for the terminal exam in writing (apart from AQA 'B' Module 3 and Scottish Standard Grade, where writing coursework is compulsory). However, a student who does badly in writing coursework is unlikely to do better in the writing terminal exam.

What can I do if a student presents me with a piece of coursework not done in controlled conditions which is obviously not his or her own work?

Should you suspect that a piece of coursework is not the student's own work, ask the student to rewrite that piece of work under 'controlled conditions', i.e. under your supervision in a detention. Alternatively, mark the work as it stands and include a note to this effect for the board. This may seem harsh on the individual candidate but helps to create a fairer situation for all candidates – yours and those from other centres. If the board suspects malpractice at your centre, it could have repercussions for all your candidates. The question of 'ownership' of work should be easier given that some coursework will be done in controlled conditions.

I keep finding similar chunks of language in their coursework – and it's not anything I've taught them. What, if anything, can I do?

Maintain a small departmental library (helpful in all your work) of coursebooks and revision guides. If you suspect inappropriate Internet use, try typing in a distinctive phrase or sentence into a good search engine, such as 'Google'.

However much I explain the rules, the students keep on handing in coursework which is not entirely their own work.

Try doing all the coursework under controlled conditions – at least for the foreseeable future.

Some students want me to extend the deadline by a fortnight so they can find more source materials, add an attractive title page and make the piece of coursework longer.

This may be counterproductive. Remind the students that pieces of work in Modern Languages are 100 words long on average and that trying to make it longer must not be at the expense of accuracy. Also, no marks are awarded for source materials and title pages. Inform them too that they will be producing the next piece of coursework in a relatively short space of time.

Can I mark the work? Can I give them feedback?

There should be no marks on the student's coursework itself. However, you may take notes about the work and give these to the student, along with the mark. However, the mark you give for each piece may not ultimately be the moderated mark awarded by the board.

> Should you wish to use the coursework for formative purposes please photocopy it before you mark it and submit the original to the board.
> *WJEC GCSE Teachers' Guide*

Can I mark more leniently at the beginning of Year 10, especially if they're doing the language ab initio?

No, the board's assessment criteria must be applied consistently throughout the course.

They have improved so much since the beginning of Year 10. Can I select pieces of coursework all done in Year 11?

Yes, as long as the three (five for WJEC) pieces selected fulfil all of the other criteria such as controlled conditions and curriculum coverage.

Our lessons are only forty minutes long and this isn't usually enough for students to complete a piece of coursework under controlled conditions. I have followed my board's instructions about keeping the work secure until they come back to complete the assignment. But what if they 'swot up' between the two lessons?

Coursework is not an 'unseen' examination, so it is difficult to regard further preparation and language practice as 'cheating' in these circumstances. You should positively encourage careful preparation of this sort at the planning stage! Look at the section 'Is that cheating?' on page 20.

When I set a writing task, I get 30 very similar pieces handed in to me. I have heard rumours that boards say it is not acceptable for the work to be similar.

There are only so many ways of expressing ideas in each language (especially at the comparatively low level of GCSE foundation tier)! In the terminal examination for writing the boards end up with many thousands of pieces of writing which all have similarities. The AQA says quite clearly:

> It is not a requirement that all candidates in a teaching group should work on different assignments, with different source material.
> *AQA 'A' Specification*

Can I tell them what the task is in advance?

Clearly you will need to if they are to prepare a draft! Most boards take the view that coursework should not be treated as an 'unseen' examination, so this allows thorough preparation of a 'known' writing task.

I didn't teach this class in Year 10 and I've inherited coursework and marks from their previous teacher.

This one can be tricky – if in any doubt about the reliability of your former colleague's marking, you need to remark. However, if you plan and standardise regularly as a team, this should not be a problem.

One of the members of my department just won't toe the line with her coursework. The worst problem is at standardisation meetings (if and when she attends) where she disputes every single mark we award for her candidates.

Colleagues need to understand that team decisions about coursework are not personal nor a judgement about standards of teaching; they relate only to the written evidence presented in the coursework. It might make it easier to standardise if you invite an informed 'outsider' to run a standardisation meeting. This could be a person appointed by your board, your LEA adviser or the Head of MFL from a neighbouring school (for whom you would return the favour). Continued non-compliance is a serious issue which should be brought to the attention of your line manager.

CiLT

Appendix

Summary of boards' requirements for GCSE Coursework/Scottish Standard Grade Writing

Board	Languages	Short course	Terminal writing exam option?	Tasks	Length
AQA 'A' Linear	French German Spanish Italian Urdu	French German Spanish	Yes	Bank of tasks, in English, differentiated by outcome	(Advisory only, total for 3 pieces) F tier – 250–300 words H tier – 400–500 words
AQA 'B' Modular Module 3	French German Spanish		Module 4 writing exam compulsory	Bank of tiered tasks, in English	Grades F/G – 40 words Grades C/D/E – 90 words Grades A*/A/B – 120 words
Edexcel	French German Spanish	French	Yes	Free choice of tasks, with option of 'units' of work	F tier – 100 words H tier – 200 words
OCR	French German Gujarati Spanish		Yes	Examples provided, but free choice, in target language	A*/A/B – 150 words C/D – 100 words E/F/G – 20–85 words
WJEC	French German Spanish		Yes	Bank of tasks, tiered, in target language, but alternatives can be submitted to board	10 sentences
SQA Standard Grade	French German Italian Russian Spanish Urdu		No	Example tasks but candidates may select their own	Credit – 100+ General – 50 Foundation – 25

CiLT

Curriculum coverage	Minimum pieces controlled	Support in controlled conditions other than dictionary	Drafting permitted?	Use of ICT	Marking?
3 themes (2 for short course)	1/3	Drafting permitted	Yes; draft of controlled conditions piece must be submitted	Permissible in all coursework	No marks or comments to be written on coursework
2 writing tasks and 1 speaking task all on different topics	0/2	N/A	Yes; all drafts must be submitted	Permissible in all coursework	No marks or comments to be written on coursework
At least 3 topic areas (2 for short course) including a mix of tasks	1/3	Dictionary only	Yes; all drafts must be submitted	Permissible in all coursework, including on-line dictionaries	Each unit is assessed globally, then marks entered on frontsheet
3 different contexts	1/3	May know sub-context in advance but not exact title	Yes, but not for controlled conditions	Not in controlled conditions	Must show how marks have been awarded, plus extra annotation if necessary
2/5 contexts	5/5	Must be completed in one sitting	No; pre-prepared material not usually permitted	Permissible in all coursework	In red pen showing clearly which tasks accomplished
3 different topics or tasks	3/3	None; final draft must be produced within 30 minutes	Yes; any sources permitted during drafting	Not permitted	Marked externally by SQA

References

Adams J (2000) 'Raising standards in MFL writing through GCSE coursework' pp1–26 in *Studies in Modern Languages Education* Vol 8, April 2000, University of Leeds

Berwick, G. and Horsfall, P. (1996) Pathfinder 28: *Making effective use of the dictionary.* CILT.

Swarbrick, A. (1998) Pathfinder 36: *More reading for pleasure in the foreign language.* CILT.

Tyson-Ward, S. (2001) *Write on … writing skills for GCSE coursework.* MLG Publishing.

 ## FURTHER READING

Adams, J. (2002) 'If you can't beat them …: the politics and impact of the GCSE and coursework' pp65–77 in Swarbrick, A. (ed) *Teaching Modern Foreign Languages in secondary schools* (OU Reader). Open University/Routledge Falmer.

Christie, C. (2002) Advanced Pathfinder 4: *Managing coursework.* CILT.

Coe, J (2001) 'What's right for writing – coursework or exam?'. *Times Educational Supplement* 19/10/2001.

 ## RESOURCES FOR COURSEWORK

The following recently-published materials all include an element of guidance and/or materials designed directly to support GCSE coursework or the development of writing skills at various ability levels. (This list is not comprehensive.)

FRENCH

Camarades (Nelson Thornes)
Equipe (Oxford University Press)
Formule X (Collins)
Métro (Heinemann)
On est fou de foot (CILT)
Voyage (Nelson Thornes)
Writing frames for GCSE coursework (Folens)

GERMAN

Fokus Deutsch für AQA (Modular) (Oxford University Press)
Logo! (Heinemann)
Mach mit! (Nelson Thornes)
Projekt Deutsch (Oxford University Press)

GUJARATI

The 100 word exercise book – Gujarati (G and W Publishing)
Colloquial Gujarati (Routledge)
Gujarati language for GCSE (Kanta Shah). Available from 020 8907 4537 or Popat Stores, 158 Ealing Rd, Wembley

ITALIAN

Forza! (Heinemann)
Saluti: writing practice for GCSE Italian (Hodder & Stoughton)
Write on … writing skills for GCSE coursework (also suitable for French, German and Spanish) (MLG Publishing)

SPANISH

En contacto: writing practice for GCSE Spanish (Hodder & Stoughton)
¡Listos! (Heinemann)
The key to GCSE Spanish writing skills (also available in French and German) (John Murray Publishing)

URDU

The 100 word exercise book (G and W Publishing)
GCSE Urdu made easy (Parvez Akhtar, Rolex Books)
Urdu for GCSE and beyond (forthcoming September 2003; e-mail: pwheeldon@blueyonder.co.uk)